Mini Beasties

Poems selected by
Michael Rosen

Illustrated by
Alan Baker

PUFFIN BOOKS

Contents

A Bug and a Flea

A bug and a flea went out to sea
Upon a reel of cotton;
The flea was drowned but the bug was found
Biting a lady's bottom.

Children's playground rhyme

Little Snail

I saw a little snail
Come down the garden walk.
He wagged his head this way . . . that
    way . . .
Like a clown in a circus.
He looked from side to side
As though he were from a different
    country.
I have always said he carries his house
    on his back . . .
To-day in the rain
I saw that it was his umbrella!

Hilda Conkling

Growing up

Little Tommy Tadpole began to weep and wail,
For little Tommy Tadpole had lost his tail,
And his mother didn't know him, as he wept upon a log;
For he wasn't Tommy Tadpole, but Mr Thomas Frog.

C.J. Dennis

Ladybug

A small speckled visitor
    wearing a crimson cape,
brighter than a cherry.
    smaller than a grape.

A polka-dotted someone
    walking on my wall,
a black-hooded lady
    in a scarlet shawl.

Joan Walsh Anglund

ladybug – ladybird

The Lazy Lizard

I'm a lazy old lizard
   Who lives at the zoo,
And catches the flies,
   And swallows them, too.

Mona Swann

8

Early Bird Does Catch the Fattest Worm

Late again
going to be late again
for school again
and I can't say
I overslept
can't blame it
on the bus
can't blame it
on the train
can't blame it
on the rain
and Granny words
buzzing in my brain
'Early bird does catch the worm,'
and I thinking
Teacher going tell me off
and I wishing
I was a bird
and teacher was a juicy worm.

John Agard

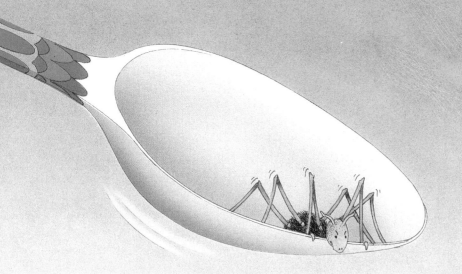

Little Miss Muffet
Sat on her tuffet,
Eating her Irish Stew.
Along came a spider
And sat down beside her,
So she ate him up too.

Children's playground rhyme

Itch

It was just a queer itch;
A tickle;
A very queer tickle;
Two tickles on top of each other;
A mosquito bite.

Gillian Hughes

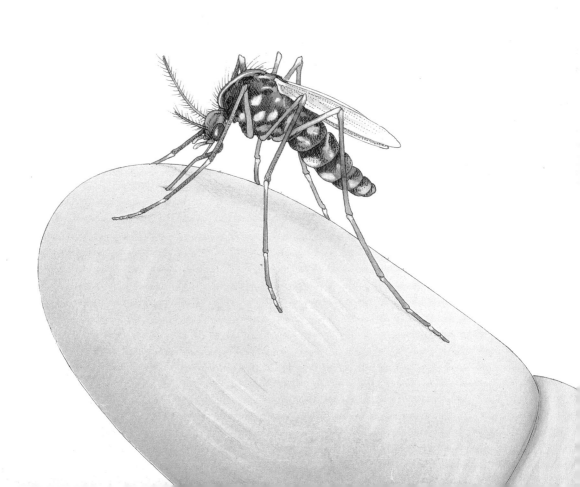

How soft the sound
Of butterflies eating!

Kyoshi

The Butterfly

I always think the butterfly
Looks best against a clear blue sky;
I do not think he looks so good
Pinned down within a box of wood.

Frank Collymore

Message from a caterpillar

Don't shake this
bough.
Don't try
to wake me
now.

In this cocoon
I've work to
do.
Inside this silk
I'm changing
things.

I'm worm-like now
but in this
dark
I'm growing
wings.

Lilian Moore

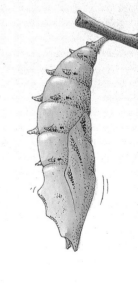

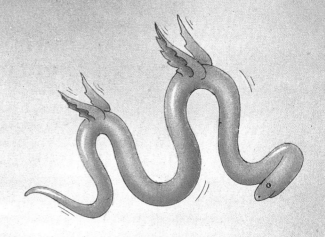

Worms can't fly,
So why do the
birds wait up
in the trees?

Roger Goffe

The Tickle Rhyme

"Who's that tickling my back?" said the wall.
   "Me," said a small
Caterpillar. "I'm learning
To crawl."

Ian Serraillier

15

Bees

Honeybees are very tricky –
Honey doesn't make them sticky.

Russell Hoban

Bees

Every bee
that
ever was
was
partly
sting
and partly
. . . buzz.

Jack Prelutsky

A city of thousands,
Yet no word is spoken.
There are great stores of gold,
But no money.
Some live imprisoned in cells,
Yet are good citizens.
Their six-legged cows,
Give sweet milk,
They have no king –
But a queen rules and serves them.

John Cunliffe

Hey, Bug!

Hey bug, stay!
Don't run away.
I know a game that we can play.

I'll hold my fingers very still
and you can climb a finger-hill.

No, no.
Don't go.

Here's a wall – a tower, too,
a tiny bug town, just for you.
I've a cookie. You have some.
Take this oatmeal cookie crumb.

Hey, bug, stay!
Hey, bug!
Hey!

Lilian Moore

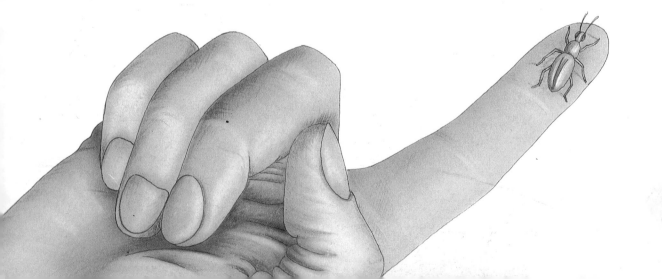

Today I saw a little worm

Today I saw a little worm
Wriggling on his belly.
Perhaps he'd like to come inside
And see what's on the Telly.

Spike Milligan

19

A Dragonfly

When the heat of the summer
Made drowsy the land,
A dragonfly came
And sat on my hand,
With its blue jointed body,
And wings like spun glass
It lit on my fingers
As though they were grass.

Eleanor Farjeon

Granny Spider

Granny Spider
Sits and knits,
She sits and knits
With all her wits.
She spins a line
Of silky twine,
And sits and knits all day.

Dennis Lee

A wasp on a nettle said: 'Coo!
We're in a right mess, me and you.
    We have got to sort out
    What this is about.
Please tell me – who's got to sting who?'

Frank Richards

Wasps

Wasps like coffee.
Syrup.
Tea.
Coca-Cola.
Butter.
Me.

Dorothy Aldis

A fly flew past Flo's flat
And a fly flew past fat Flo.
Is the fly that flew past Flo
The same fly that flew past fat Flo's flat?

Anon. adapted by Michael Rosen

Earwig

The horny-goloch is an awesome beast,
Soople an scaly;
It has twa horns, an a hantle o feet,
An a forkie tailie.

Anon.

horny-goloch – earwig
soople – supple
hantle – lots

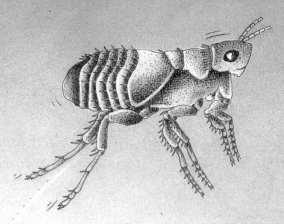

The Flea

And here's the happy, bounding flea –
You cannot tell the he from she.
The sexes look alike, you see;
But she can tell and so can he.

Roland Young

The Red Gown

The red gown we see is like a butterfly
A red gown that catches the eye
The red gown we see is like a butterfly

Red gown dancing in joy
A red gown that catches the eye
The red gown we see is like a buttefly

Red gown dancing in joy
A red gown that catches the eye
The red gown we see is like a butterfly
Red gown dancing in joy

Jimmy Murray

From *The honey-ant men's love song and other Aboriginal song poems* edited by R.M.W. Dixon and Martin Duwell 1990, University of Queensland Press, Australia.

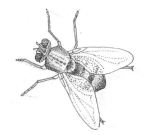

Oh the Toe-Test!

The fly, the fly,
in the wink of an eye,
can taste with his feet
if the syrup is sweet
or the bacon is salty.
Oh is it his fault he
gets toast on his toes
as he tastes as he goes?

Norma Farber

27

I'm an ant
and a gi–ant.
I'm a gi–ant
to an ant,
but
I'm an ant
to a gi–ant.

Pam Brewster

I did not touch him

On the way to school David and I spied a millipede, almost
  under my feet.
I was counting worms all the way down the road.
We had counted two hundred and fifteen by the time we saw
  the millipede.
He was a pale yellow, with little black feet.
I did not touch him but left him on his way
And made sure I didn't crush him.
Some creatures I crush without bothering
But not this one.
I hadn't seen one before.
I turned back and saw him trying to climb a rain-slithery fence,
But all his legs didn't help him,
And he dropped back to the path,
Feet-in-the-air,
Helpless.

Stuart Wilson

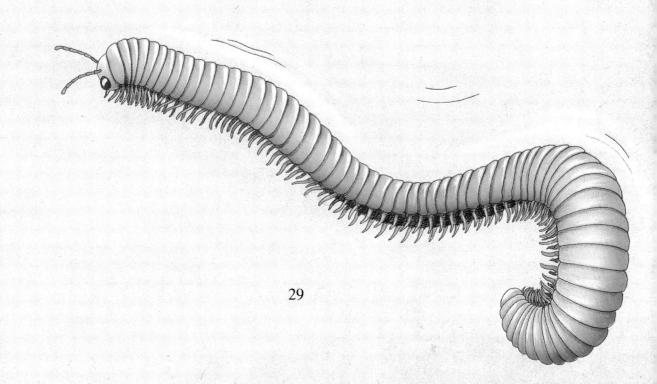

A Wee Little Worm

A wee little worm in a hickory-nut
   Sang, happy as he could be,
'O I live in the heart of the whole round world,
   And it all belongs to me!'

James Whitcomb Riley

Chisoku

The face of the dragonfly
Is practically nothing
But eyes.

Japan, Seventeenth century
Trans. R.H. Blyth

Index of First Lines

Acknowledgements

Page 5 from *Those First Affections*, collected and introduced by Timothy Rogers, Routledge, London. **Page 6** from *A Book for Kids* by C.J. Dennis. Reproduced by kind permission of Angus and Robertson Publishers. **Page 7** from *Morning is a Little Child* by Joan Walsh Anglund. Copyright © 1969 by Joan Walsh Anglund, Harcourt Brace Jovanovich Inc., USA. **Page 8** from *Trippingly on the Tongue* by Mona Swann, Macmillan. **Page 9** from *Say It Again, Granny!* 20 poems from Caribbean proverbs by John Agard, The Bodley Head, London. **Page 11** from *Those First Affections* collected and introduced by Timothy Rogers, Routledge. **Page 12** (top) from *Don't Tell the Scarecrow* and other Japanese Poems, by Issa, Yayu, Kikaku and other Japanese poets, Scholastic Book Services, USA. **Page 13** from *Little Raccoon and Poems from the Woods* by Lilian Moore. Atheneum Publishers, USA. Copyright © 1975 by Lilian Moore, reprinted by permission of Marian Reiner for the author. **Page 14** from *Kidstuff* by Roger Goffe © Roger Goffe 1980, ITV Books Ltd. Reprinted by permission of Syndicated Humour Ltd. **Page 15** from *The Monster Horse* copyright © 1950 by Ian Serraillier. Published by Oxford University Press. Reproduced with permission from the author. **Page 16** (top) from *Egg Thoughts and Other Frances Songs* by Russell Hoban, Faber and Faber Ltd. **Page 16** (bottom) from *Zoo Doings* by Jack Prelutsky; copyright © 1983 Jack Prelutsky, by permission of Greenwillow Books, a division of William and Morrow and Co., Inc., New York. **Page 17** from *"Riddles" 1, Standing on a Strawberry* by John Cunliffe. Andre Deutsch. **Page 18** from *I Feel the Same Way* by Lilian Moore, copyright © 1967 by Lilian Moore. Reprinted by permission of Marian Reiner for the author. Published by Atheneum. **Page 19** from *Silly Verse for Kids* by Spike Milligan, Dobson Books Ltd. Copyright clearance granted by Spike Milligan Productions Ltd. **Page 20** from *Silver Sand and Snow* published by Michael Joseph Ltd. Reproduced by permission of David Higham Associates Ltd. **Page 21** from *"Granny Spider"* by Dennis Lee, from *Jelly Belly* by Dennis Lee, published by Macmillan of Canada, with the permission of the author. **Page 22** (top) from *Limerick Delight* chosen by E.O. Parrott, Puffin Books. Reproduced with permission from the author. **Page 22** (bottom) from *Is Anybody Hungry?* by Dorothy Aldis, the Putnam Publishing Group. **Page 25** from *Not for Children* by Roland Young. Doubleday and Company, Inc. **Page 26** *"The Red Gown"* by Jimmy Murray from *The honey-ant men's love song and other Aboriginal song poems.* Edited by R.M.W. Dixon and Martin Duwell, 1990 University of Queensland Press, Australia. **Page 27** from *Never say ugh to a bug* by Norma Farber, William Morrow & Company, Inc. **Page 29** from *My World: poems from Living Language* edited by Joan Griffiths, BBC Books. **Page 31** from *Haiku* by R.H. Blyth, The Hokuseido Press, Tokyo, Japan.

While every effort has been made to trace the copyright holders, in some cases it has proved impossible. The publishers apologise for this apparent negligence.